BITS and Pieces

a Memoir

Edward W. Lull

∞ INFINITY
PUBLISHING

All rights reserved. No part of this book shall be reproduced or transmitted in any form or by any means, electronic, mechanical, magnetic, photographic including photocopying, recording or by any information storage and retrieval system, without prior written permission of the publisher. No patent liability is assumed with respect to the use of the information contained herein. Although every precaution has been taken in the preparation of this book, the publisher and author assume no responsibility for errors or omissions. Neither is any liability assumed for damages resulting from the use of the information contained herein.

Copyright © 2011 by Edward W. Lull
Cover Art by Elizabeth Randolph

ISBN 0-7414-6794-1
Library of Congress Control Number: 2011934899

Printed in the United States of America

Published September 2011

INFINITY PUBLISHING
1094 New DeHaven Street, Suite 100
West Conshohocken, PA 19428-2713
Toll-free (877) BUY BOOK
Local Phone (610) 941-9999
Fax (610) 941-9959
Info@buybooksontheweb.com
www.buybooksontheweb.com

Table of Contents

Dedication v
Introduction vii

Part One - The Early Years 1
Train Under Attack 2
Terror Dance 3
The Fire 4
The War Comes Home 6
When Times Were Hard 8
Victory Garden 10
Brotherly Love 12
Gray's Woods 13
A Bloody Saturday 14
That Was My Dad 16
Algebraic Mystique 18
The Sly Pond Swim 19
Arlene 21
Secret Love 23
The Day the Skinny Lab Died 25

Part Two - The Middle Years 29
God's Call 31
The Burdens of the Fish and Wildlife Officer 32
The Escape Tower 39
Troubled Waters 41
Where's My Oscar?! 44
Christmas Party 50
Just Getting There Was Half the Fun 51
A Special Christmas 58
The Present 60
Incomplete Spring 61
Trouble on the Trail 63
On My Mother's Passing 64
The Ballad of Deliverance or Dropping a
 Daughter Off at College 67

Part Three - **The Later Years** 71
The Hardwood Ball 72
The Love-Hate Game 73
A Dizzy Day 74
Joyless Journey 75
The Leader 76
My Oval Landscape 77
Echo(of a)cardiogram 80
Fairway Folly 81
On My 50th High School Reunion 83
A Golden Journey 85
Mid-Winter Encounter 86
On Visiting Stuarts Draft Middle School 87
Witness to the Crime 88
The "I"s Have It 89
I Am in Love - Again 90
About the Author 92

List of Figures

i-1	Ed and Evelyn's Children	vi
1-1	The Lull Boys, Circa 1942	27
2-1	James Patrick Lull	30
2-2	Lieutenant Ed, OIC USS Roncador	43
2-3	Ed and Evelyn – Party-goers	51
2-4	Lieutenant-Commander Ed, At Work	53
2-5	Richard Adelbert Lull and Son Ed	62
2-6	Marybelle Brooks Lull and Son Ed	66
2-7	Commander Ed, Awarded a Medal	69
3-1	Grandchildren and Others Await the Gun	79
3-2	Ed & Evelyn, June 4, 1955	84
3-3	Ed & Evelyn, June 4, 2005	84
3-4	Fourth Generation of Love	90
3-5	The Children and Spouses	91
3-6	The Grandchildren	91
3-7	Edward Warren Lull, Circa 1937	93

Dedication

Our time on this earth consists of a series of life-changing experiences - some of us many, some not so many. Geographic moves, schools, careers, marriage, retirement, etc. all present challenges and opportunities that require that we adapt - that we rise to the challenges and seize the opportunities. We experience highs and lows - successes and failures - but we learn from all on the road to aging.

On looking back, and that's what a memoir forces us to do, it didn't take me long to sort through my memories to identify the most significant and rewarding life-changing event. It towers above the rest. It is - having children and sharing the parenting experience with my partner and love of my life: my wife, Evelyn. It started in sadness when we lost our first child, James Patrick. However, the experience rebounded in 1958 with the birth of our daughter. Three years later we had a son, then two years after that, another son. Providing love and guidance to these children brought challenges - but great joy to us. Seeing them mature into loving and responsible adults brought us great satisfaction. However, as we now see the results of their parenting, our eight wonderful grandchildren, our lives, indeed, are full.

So, I am pleased to dedicate this book to the stars of my most significant life-changing experience, Ed and Evelyn's children:

Jeanne Lull Hopke
Edward W. Lull, Jr.
James Michael Lull

**Figure i-1. Ed & Evelyn's Children
Ed Jr., Jeanne, Jim**

Introduction

This book is a collection of poems and essays about incidents in my life. I assume they were significant, because I remember them with a fair amount of clarity 50 - 60 - 70 years later. The stories I related in essay form contained more information than I was comfortable constraining myself to the disciplines of poetry. I believe they flow better in conversational English.

The book is divided into three sections:

The Early Years - From earliest memories to college times.
The Middle Years - Covering career and parenting years.
The Later Years - Retirement times.

Memoirs need not have the form nor the substance of an autobiography. Whereas the autobiography is history, requiring research and accuracy, the memoir is more a series of remembrances. If the memoir is merely legacy writing to provide the reader with more insights into the life of the author, there need be no real linkages between the incidents included other than that they occurred to the author. Why not use poetry as a medium?

Many poets use incidents in their lives as subjects for narrative poems. Poets are free to employ their special writing skills to create memoirs of a unique type. That is what I attempted in assembling this book.

BITS AND PIECES

Part One

The Early Years

Train Under Attack

On hands and knees,
in a line, playing train:
Sonny, at 5, the engineer,
then Bobby,4, finally Eddie, 3.
Snaking along in the side yard grass,
they heard a thump nearby.
Sonny looked up and saw
a Negro boy, in the street,
reaching down to fetch another
stone to throw at the cortège.

Sonny maneuvered the human train
toward the side door at as high a speed
as he could crawl. The caboose didn't keep up -
and *thwack* - the stone hit Eddie in the head.
He sat in the grass, wailing; Sonny
and Bobbie dragged him in the house.

Mother tended to Eddie's wound and
calmed him down. She laid down a law:
"Whenever you see one of ***those people***,
you are to come inside - immediately.
You never know what ***they*** will do!"

Mother was born and raised in Canada,
and with her move to Pennsylvania,
she brought her great love of children,
her convent-taught Catholic faith,
and her nurse-trained healing arts with her.
Where her biases came from, I never knew,
but they were part of her
throughout her life.

Terror Dance

It was late afternoon;
Mother was working on dinner, and said:
"Eddie, go down and get me a jar
of string beans from the cupboard."
Dutifully I opened the door
to the dimly-lit cellar, and started
down the rough-hewn steps toward
the dirt-floor below.

On the fourth step, my face was engulfed
by an invisible spider web - I SCREAMED!
My feet went up and down in rapid succession
on the step; my fists were pumping the air.
With a great crescendo I yelled:
"HE'S BITING ME!"
(I subsequently dubbed this my terror dance.)

Quickly, two strong arms whisked me up
to the lighted kitchen where I expected
to die in peace. I didn't - but I cried a lot.
It took two parents a while to calm me down,
and my older brother, with an unsympathetic
shake of his head, went into another room
where it was quieter.

A lifetime aversion to spiders - no a **deep fear**
of spiders - was born that day, even though
during the incident I never saw a spider.

The Fire

My brother Bob, 10, and I, 9, enjoyed hiking. One day Bob proposed that we explore *the jungle*, a section of woods filled with trees and vines that resembled a scene from a *Tarzan* movie.

It was sunny and the hike there went quickly; it was only a couple of miles from home. As we entered the forest the dense growth hid the sun and made hiking slow and tiring. Suddenly we broke into a clearing with no trees, just a small field of straw. While resting, Bob produced a book of matches, and said: "Let's build a campfire." He must have had the campfire idea in his mind from the start, or why else would he have brought matches? Instead of stating the obvious, of what a bad idea it was, I said: "Good idea!"

Bob found a circular strip of metal from an old wooden barrel, and laid it in the middle of the field, announcing that the ring would prevent the campfire from spreading. Remember, this was a field of straw! The campfire looked rather nice - for about ten seconds - after which we both began stomping on the flames that failed to appreciate the fact that they were supposed to remain within the ring. Within a minute, we were running full throttle to avoid the hell we had created. On the way home, we heard the fire engines on the way to the scene. We agreed that there was no possibility that this incident could end well. Our strategy: tell Mother everything and depend on her mercy and protection.

Mother listened patiently, asked a few questions, then said:
"Both of you go to your rooms, close the doors, and stay
until I call you. I can't promise anything, but I will talk
to the police **when** they come." The two hours I spent behind
that closed door reminded me that I was a felon, and could
spend the night in a cell. I stared at my bedroom door,
wondering if the next person to come through
would be my Mother with a ruler,
my Father with fire in his eyes,
or a policeman carrying handcuffs.

When Mother called us to dinner, we came downstairs;
Dad greeted us in the hall and said quietly:
"I hope you boys learned something today."
I don't recall of ever speaking again of this,
but have marveled at the restraint and wisdom
my parents showed: quite a lesson in parenting.

The War Comes Home

"The Japs bombed Pearl Harbor."
I knew the news was bad.
"Where's Pearl Harbor?" I asked my Dad.
"In Hawaii - across the Pacific."
A fourth grader finds that very far away.
"Is that in our country?"
"Well technically - no, but ..."
He droned on a while, but
what I heard was "no."

Next year, the war talk among adults
was done in muted tones.
That's OK. I had more important things to think about.
A family near us had two older boys:
one, a junior named Phil,
a bright and talented three-season athlete.
We all looked up to Phil.
His brother - a tall skinny redhead - was a senior;
friendly to the kids - everyone called him Gander.

One day next summer my brother announced:
"Did you know Gander got drafted?"
I wondered how gawky Gander would do as a soldier,
but I felt the war had just gotten closer.
The term Midway was heard regularly;
I think the war was going better.
In the town square the names of the servicemen
were listed on a large board;
I enjoyed going by it and seeing Gander's name.
Somehow, it made me feel part of it.

One day, after school I went to the drug store;
my dime bought my favorite: pineapple milkshake.
On the way home, I went by the serviceman's board, as usual.
By Gander's name, there was a gold star.

A GOLD STAR. OH, NO. I knew what that meant.
Normally, pineapple milkshakes and I got along fine.
But not that day.
Dad said boys my age don't cry. I did anyway.
The war had come home.

When Times Were Hard

We entered town on streets of rustic brick
and through an arch of regal elms.
Our journey near its end,
our new home close at hand.
My hopes had turned to trepidation now:
why did we have to move so far away?

Our home in Pennsylvania was quite small,
but I had lived there all my life.
A war was on and times were hard,
but Dad found work, though not nearby.
There was no choice for us but move up north
and start a new life near the Berkshire hills.

We drove slowly down Corliss Avenue,
our old green Chevy wheezing from the trip.
Dad stopped the car in front of our new home,
and anxiety turned to joy as we viewed
a great white house set back from the street
with lots of space for four young boys to play.

On moving day the neighbors gathered 'round
to welcome us and make us feel at home.
My Dad had clearly picked a place with us in mind
to ease the sadness caused by leaving friends behind.
The warmth that Greenwich showed us that day
defined the lure of rural, small town life.

The next few years were all a boy could want,
considering that folks said times were hard.
I swam and fished at Pine Woods on the Battenkill;
climbed each crag and crossed each stream at Sherman's Rocks.
But most of all I hiked throughout Gray's Woods
and learned to ski there on the tallest hill.
The war still on, my Dad was called to go

and build air fields on some Aleutian isle.
Our lives went on, but things were changing now;
Dad's absence left some voids we had to fill.
We did our chores and tried to ease the pain
that Mom endured with Dad so far away.

Dad's safe return brought much relief and joy,
our family together once again.
But jobs were very scarce and times still hard
with rent and food and all now costing more.
The atmosphere of change engulfed our home;
the bitter truth was difficult to grasp.

With sadness in our hearts we bid farewell
to home and friends - that segment of our lives
that fostered values that we knew would last.
Our fam'ly lives were never quite the same,
with city life and different friends and schools.
But we grew up when times, indeed, were hard.

Victory Garden

The concept that planting a vegetable garden
in rural upstate New York
could help win a war overseas
completely escaped me.
We weren't eliminating the enemy,
nor were we feeding our soldiers.
We planted, we weeded, we fertilized, we harvested;
then we ate like real farmers all winter.
Perhaps someday I'll understand this war thing.

Corn was easy to plant and tend.
I had studied how Indians planted corn in mounds;
five seed kernels and one dead fish per hill.
We planted in rows - and left out the fish.
When the corn grew, it had strong stalks,
green tasseled soldiers, never intimidated by weeds.
Corn-on-the-cob was the best (even with oleo).

I love carrots, especially raw,
crunchy, crisp, and sweet as jujubes,
but what a pain to grow.
The seeds are as small as pepper flakes,
and you plant them so shallow - you barely cover them.
They germinate far too close,
so they must be thinned - terribly tedious.
Weeds sprout up to dominate the tender plants,
but pulling a weed without uprooting several plants -
difficult! But what would a pot roast be without them?

My Dad showed me how to cut seed potatoes
to ensure that each section contained a promising eye.
Potato hills were easy to keep tidy with a hoe,
and digging them up at the end was exciting;
you never know how many you'd find in a hill.
Beets were like carrots, no fun - too much work.
When you pulled them up, they bled on your hands;
I didn't even like the taste of beets.

A damp spring produced a bountiful crop of peas;
I ate them raw out of the pods.
We really over-killed on string beans;
Mother canned almost a hundred quart Ball jars.

I guess I did enjoy the gardening experience
and it must have been successful:
you know, winning the war, and all.

Brotherly Love

The summer after moving to Greenwich
in Upstate New York, my two older brothers
and I had established good friendships with
other boys in the neighborhood. A group of us
went swimming in a peaceful cove in the fast-flowing
Battenkill River. I hadn't learned to swim yet.

Noting that the boys could walk across the outer
perimeter of the cove, I reasoned that I could walk
across the cove closer in to shore. This was
the first time I had been to the cove - and I was wrong.

About halfway between the outer perimeter and
the shore, I slipped into the water and began a dog
paddle. About halfway across, I tired, stopped
my stroke and let my feet sink; they did not touch
bottom. My head sank beneath the surface; I hadn't
taken a breath. I panicked! I began gasping for air
and flailing around. The prospect of drowning seized
me. Suddenly someone grabbed me and tried to pull
me out. Instead, with my adrenalin flowing, I pulled
him under. In a blur of terror, a strong hand came under
my chin, pulled my head above water, and towed me to
shore. I was saved by a Boy Scout with life saving training.
The one who got to me first was my brother Bob.

Thoroughly shaken by the experience, that day I committed
myself to: Learn to swim, I did; join the Boy Scouts, I did;
learn life saving techniques, I did. As time went on the key
part of the incident that emerged was not that an older,
skilled
life saver had pulled me out with apparent ease, it was that
the first one to get to me, and risk his life to save me was
my brother.
I haven't forgotten. I never will.

Gray's Woods

I never knew the man named Mr. Gray;
His wealth included land and cars and goods.
To me, a boy of twelve or so,
I didn't really care, although
When hiking I was home within Gray's Woods.

From town I'd walk across the fields of hay,
Where Queen Anne's Lace and Goldenrod abound.
A waist-high wall of rocks and shale
Was easy for a boy to scale,
Then on across a stream and up a mound.

As I approached the woods I saw the play
Of squirrels racing up and 'round a tree.
A crow atop a lofty limb
Announces to his flock that HIM,
Our guest is here again. No need to flee.

I climbed the hills as I have done each day
That I have spent in solitude and peace.
The sky so blue, the leaves so green,
The water clear; and life's serene,
Until disturbed by honking of the geese.

Forgive me Mr. Gray, but I could stay
Forever in this place I love as home,
Where huge rocks were like temples grand
The tall oaks guarding all the land,
And birds and furry friends were free to roam.

As afternoon wears on a taunting jay
Reminds me that the day is nearly done;
Reluctantly I leave the glade
And cross the fields in gold arrayed,
To end my day beneath the setting sun.

A Bloody Saturday

Greenwich had an early November snow
in my sixth grade year and Chester,
my Polish, 14-year old classmate,
invited me to come to his farm
for a Saturday afternoon. He would
show me around the farm, and later,
we could hike in the surrounding woods.
My Dad drove me there, and I had
a brief tour of farm life.

Chester's father was out, and when we
were ready to hike, Chester produced
two 22-caliber rifles for us to carry.
His mother delivered some not-to-gentle
words in Polish, probably voicing opposition
to taking the rifles out. Chester responded
in kind, and off we went, rifles in hand;
he had a clip gun, mine was a single shot.

After hiking through the snow for an hour
we were heading back toward the farm house.
Since we hadn't fired the guns yet, Chester
set up a piece of wood for a target and we
backed off and fired a few rounds. He then said
we should unload and trudge the final hundred
yards or so to his home. I removed my shell
from the chamber and he removed his clip.
He forgot to remove the round in the chamber.

Chester started fooling around with his rifle, and
CRACK his rifle fired; a searing pain in my groin
sat me down in the snow. Chester panicked; I said
"Go, get help!" He ran to the house, screaming, and
soon returned with his father. They half carried,
half dragged me through the slippery snow, finally
reaching the house, and the warmth of their parlor.
Chester's 18-year old sister had called my folks.
As they laid me on the couch, the sister said
in a commanding voice, "Don't touch his foot."
She had noticed my bloody shoe. I touched
my groin and groaned, "I'm shot here."
Chester's sister hit the floor in a dead faint.

My memory is rather fuzzy at this point,
but my parents arrived shortly thereafter,
loaded me in the car, and headed for
Cambridge Hospital at speeds that
dirt roads were not built to handle.
I later learned that I had lost two quarts
of blood, but I survived. The bullet had
severed some nerves, but no arteries, and
lodged close to the upper part of the left femur.
Doctors concluded that they could do more
damage removing the bullet than it would
cause if they left it where it was. So,
to this day, I carry a souvenir of that bloody
Saturday, when I failed to "dodge a bullet."

That Was My Dad

One day a year, on Father's Day
I know I must recall
through fog of years, I wonder if
I knew my Dad at all.
Who was my Dad?

About six feet and large of girth,
he sold seeds, bulbs, and plants.
In high school he'd have done OK,
but never got the chance.
That was my Dad.

Depression years and pay was low
the times for all were hard.
He took a risky part-time job:
a penitentiary guard.
That was my Dad.

To earn some more he undertook
piano-moving work.
He had his children to support;
hard work he'd never shirk.
That was my Dad.

Republican through to the core:
a self-reliant gent.
He had no use for whiners who
could never be content.
That was my Dad.

That April day in forty-five
when I had come inside,
his face reflected tragedy:
our President had died.
That was my Dad.

We *saw* them honor FDR
through radio's mystique.
With sadness I had never seen,
a tear ran down his cheek.
Was that my Dad?

He died so many years ago
I don't remember much.
We never spoke of love, I know,
just work and sports and such.
God bless my Dad!

Algebraic Mystique

Erasers all clapped, board clean,
my job - honor - done.
I always competed for the top spot in the class,
but John Rutledge and Lila Tomlinson
also wanted that distinction.
It was good - and friendly - competition;
none of us dominated the other two.

Strolling down the hall past a seventh grade class,
I noted that the board had not been cleaned.
Peering through the window I saw
a long string of letters and numbers.
They must have finished the day with algebra;
I recognized it because my seventh grade brother
complained about it so much. He said
it was like arithmetic, except they used
A's and B's, X's and Y's. I liked math
and looked forward to taking it next year.

At the bottom of the glob of confusing characters
on the seventh grade board was the line:
$X = 7$. I was elated; the walk home
seemed to go especially fast that afternoon.
At dinner, I mentioned that I was ready to begin
algebra in September, especially since I had
advance understanding of the subject.
"How's that?" Bob inquired. "Well,"
I proudly announced, "I already know
that $X = 7$." Bob and Dad exchanged
a knowing glance, then continued eating.

I wondered why.

The Sly Pond Swim

As a skinny, 13-year old Boy Scout,
I was tenting at Camp Wakpominee
in the Adirondacks for the second time.
My brother and two friends planned to swim
the length of Sly Pond, then back to camp.
The invited me to join them; never being one
to turn down a dare or challenge, I agreed.
It was estimated to be a mile and a quarter,
far further than I ever swam before.
What was I thinking?!

Five of us boarded the safety boat that
would accompany us. At the end of the lake
four of us slipped into the water and began.
All of us started with a crawl (free style) stroke,
but before swimming much time or distance,
I tired and had to resort to less strenuous strokes
(side or back strokes). Soon I was lagging the others.
As time went on, the distance between us grew.
As the leaders approached the turning point where
they would change course and do the final leg,
I could hardly see that they were still doing the crawl.
The scout in the "safety" boat must have thought
his mission was to outpace all swimmers
back to camp; he was no use to me.

When I lolly-gagged around the turn, I saw the others
leaving the water, walking toward tents, the boat tied up.
I was now alone on Sly Pond, stick-like arms lead weights,
and a feeling in my stomach bordering on panic. I rolled
onto my back trying to relax and recommit myself
to finishing. From there on, I stayed with the slow
but less demanding strokes, always moving forward.

My glacial pace finally got me to the pier. I didn't have strength enough to pull myself out, so I went hand over hand until my feet touched bottom. The fear had been replaced with anger. Looking for my brother I wanted to accuse him of attempted fratricide. However, when I found him, remembering that he was my brother, I said:
"Sorry I was so slow out there."

Arlene

When I started my college career
at New York State College for Teachers,
I was an "under:"
under-funded and under-motivated.
I didn't aspire to be a teacher, and
I had no income except for what
I could earn by working at night.

The bright spot of that semester
was Arlene, a good-looking blonde;
we clicked from day one.
However, sleeping through every
world history lecture I attended
did not bode well for academic success.

On a cold December in 1950, it was clear
the conflict in Korea was not winding down,
but was exploding into something no one
expected when we got involved the
preceding June. My two older brothers
joined the Navy the day after Christmas,
and I announced that I would not return
to school for the second semester.

I finished the semester so I could at least
leave with a few college credits, then left
for home in Cambridge. Leaving college was easy;
leaving Arlene wasn't. After enlisting in the Navy
I had to wait for swearing in until the Boot Camp
at Great Lakes had time to open another section;
the Korean conflict was now in high gear.
I kept in touch with Arlene, but we didn't see
each other for more than a month. Finally,
in February I was called, was sworn in,
and boarded a train headed for Great Lakes.

It was evening when we had a brief stop-over
in Albany. I was just getting to know some
of my fellow recruits, when the sergeant in charge
of our group called my name: "Lull, you have
a visitor on the platform - make it short."
Glancing out the window as I was heading
for an exit, I saw standing on the platform,
hair blowing in the breeze, and looking God-awful sexy,
was Arlene. With catcalls following me,
I bounded off the train and locked up
in a purely passionate embrace for the
three or four minutes we had before:
"BOARD" was called by the conductor.

As I walked back down the aisle to my seat,
I sensed an atmosphere of awe emanating
from my fellow "boots." I enjoyed a level
of respect from these soon-to-be sailors
that I could not have achieved alone.

Incidentally, that was the last time I ever saw Arlene.

Secret Love

A Naval Academy plebe's life is monastic - then I saw a
movie featuring Pier Angeli.

I never told a soul about
my love affair with Pier.
Some secrets just should not get out,
especially not here.

A plebe midshipman then I was
when first I saw her smile.
The movie matters not, because
'twas I she would beguile.

My closest friend soon knew that I
was mooning over her.
He told me I should not be shy,
a meeting should occur.

Two months from then we'd be allowed
to date at our first dance.
"Just ask her! I bet she'd be proud
to come and take a chance."

My ardor oozing from my pen,
(too much I'd not presume)
inviting her to come here when
azaleas were in bloom.

Our dance would be a fine affair,
the debutantes would come.
My date would be the cutest there;
my heartstrings she would strum.

Excitement grew as days went on
until I realized,
acceptance time had come and gone;
my dreams had been capsized.

I never held her in my arms;
her lips I never kissed.
But then, she never knew **my** charms -
just think how much she missed!

But don't tell anyone!!

The Day the Skinny Lab Died

Electrical engineering, a subject area we called *Skinny*,
was not my strong suit at the Academy.
I struggled with it academically, and had to work
just to get a passing grade.

The final hurdle to clear was the practical exam
we referred to as the Skinny Lab.
The process that would be followed was this:
as our section arrives at the lab,
each of us would be handed a slip of paper
with our individual assignment on it.
Each of us would be expected to go to our station,
wire up whatever our assignment was,
apply the power, and pray that it runs.

The night before, I studied with a few classmates,
reviewing the half-dozen or so possibilities
that our assignment could be. The final one
I studied was, perhaps, the easiest -
a shunt-wound motor. I acknowledged
that my three greatest fears were:
spiders, snakes, and 250-volts.
Tomorrow, the last would be first.

As I walked into the lab the next morning,
the prof handed me the dreaded assignment slip.
Acting cool, I casually glanced at it - and saw
Shunt-Wound Motor. Inwardly, my confidence
surged. I went to my station and surveyed
the equipment I had at my disposal. *Go slow*,
I told myself, remembering that I was dealing with
250-volts.

By the time I completed my wiring,
many of my smarter classmates had
completed their projects, and the lab
was filled with the music of dozens
of whirring motors and generators.
Ready to add my motor to the chorus,
I confidently thrust my power lead into
the 250-volt bus in the floor. A small
lightning bolt leaped from the bus.
The symphony went: rrrrrrrrrr - then silence.
The lights went out; the profs ran
from station to station to locate the problem,
but everyone's exam was over.
I had blown the main circuit breaker for the building.

Fifty-some years later I was playing golf
with another Academy alum about twenty
years younger than I, when this incident came to my mind.
I told him the story, and as I was finishing
he was looking at me with a huge grin.
"So you're the one! When I went through
that lab, the profs were still telling the story.
All midshipmen have heard it."
Yep, I said, *I'm the one that did it.*
Later I was thinking that those
who came after me never knew:
I was selected to represent my classmates
on the Brigade Honor Committee;
led my company cross-country team;
quarterbacked the company touch football team;
pitched for the company softball team;
was the final set 11th Company Commander.
But they had all learned about
the day the skinny lab died.
Walking down the 18th fairway, my stride
took on a bit of a swagger - I thought:
I am a legend.

Figure 1-1. The Lull Boys, Circa 1942
Richard (Sonny), Edward (Eddie), Robert (Bobby)

BITS AND PIECES

Part Two

The Middle Years

**Figure 2-1. James Patrick Lull, b. 5/17/57 - d. 5/18/57
Fort Rosecrans National Cemetery, San Diego**

God's Call

The sun rose with a special glow that day,
the long anticipated time had passed.
And now my love had painful work to do,
a task she undertook with verve and grace...
The time had come!

Enveloped by a wave of joyous thoughts,
we dreamt about the things that were to be:
the wonders of the life that lay ahead.
Our first born child - a son - a gift from God...
And he was here!

The second day the clouds had dimmed the glow,
our happiness was tempered with concern.
But hopeful parents never dream the worst,
we knew our little son could make it through...
Then he was gone!

He never knew his mother's loving touch,
he never saw the beauty of the sky.
How could a little life be ended thus?
And we be left behind to wonder why...
We felt alone!

The pain of loss can leave eternal scars,
we never even brought him to our home.
But years and wisdom helped us understand:
God's plan for him was different from our own...
*And he **is** home!*

The Burdens of the Fish and Wildlife Officer

My initial assignment as a freshly-minted ensign, U.S. Navy was Main Propulsion Assistant aboard USS Colahan (DD-658) in San Diego. My first few months were spent becoming acclimated with the ship in general, the engineering plant in particular, learning the names and skills of my division's personnel, and adjusting to the life of a seagoing sailor. I knew that in a few months we would be deploying to the Western Pacific on a six-month cruise. There would be much preparation required before we took in all lines and headed toward the sunset. One part of that preparation came as a surprise just two weeks before departure.

Colahan was one of four ships in Destroyer Division 172, which, when coupled with the four destroyers of Division 171, formed Destroyer Squadron 17, the Seahorse Squadron. That label was attached when the squadron was formed shortly after World War II. I regale you with this trivia only because of its relevance to my story. At an officers' meeting in the wardroom two weeks before deployment, the Captain announced that he wanted to have a fish tank installed in the wardroom and to inhabit the tank with a few seahorses; he obviously felt the Squadron Commander would be quite impressed with his creativity. That was the nature of my Commanding Officer. He thought that it should come under the purview of the Engineering Department, and said: "Lull, make it happen."

Although I had seen pictures of seahorses, I don't believe I had actually seen a real seahorse, let alone had any idea how or where they live, what they eat, or how to treat them. What I did know for sure, after four years at the Naval Academy was how to respond to this weird bit of senior stupidity. Collecting all my creativity, I replied: "Aye, aye, sir." My boss, the Chief Engineer, struggling to keep from breaking up, said: "Mr. Lull will assume the position of Fish and Wildlife Officer". While the other officers guffawed, I recalled a line that Zane Grey used in several of his westerns: "He smiled without mirth."

Had Wikipedia been available in those days, I'd have learned that the taxonomy of the *genus hippocampus* contains 47 varieties of these critters. Mercifully I did not have that information to further mess with my mind. The first task was to determine where in the wardroom would a fish tank fit and what logistics problems needed to be overcome to make an installation feasible that could safely remain in place on a rocking and rolling destroyer. Once the tank purchase and installation was underway, I needed to get to the main attraction - the seahorses. I did a quick study so I wouldn't look too dumb when I went to procure them.

Let me tell you a little about these creatures. They swim upright by rapidly fluttering a dorsal fin, and steering with pectoral fins located behind their eyes. They are normally seen resting because they are poor swimmers. They have long snouts that they use to suck up food; their eyes operate independent of one another. Quite interesting - and very weird - is how they reproduce. When mating, the female deposits eggs in a brood pouch on the front side of the male seahorse. The male fertilizes the eggs and supplies them with prolactin. The brood pouch provides oxygen as well as an incubator environment for the eggs to hatch within the pouch. The gestation period is usually two to four weeks. When the very fat male finally expels the 100-200 fully developed seahorses, the parents have little to do with the offspring; they are good to go. Now here is the tough part. The male typically gives birth at night, and by morning is ready for the next batch of eggs. The guy is a sex machine, as is his funny-looking babe.

When I located a pet store that had a wide variety of fish for sale, I asked about little seahorses; they said they stocked the dwarf variety of seahorses. I described what I was looking for and gave her the size of the tank we were installing. The woman waiting on me seemed to be quite knowledgeable about these little fish; she assured me that the tank was large enough to house a few seahorses. She also informed me of the temperature ranges necessary as well as the importance of keeping a bubbling air supply going in the tank. I asked her what they ate, and she replied - brine shrimp. When I told her we would be away from San Diego for a long time and asked where would I get brine shrimp to feed the fish. She pulled a box off a shelf and told me this supply of brine shrimp eggs would hold me for a year. "Just drop some eggs in water and they will hatch - then you scoop the live shrimp out and drop them into the tank." "One moment," I said, "What am I scooping the live shrimp from?" "The brine shrimp tank," she said. "I don't have a brine shrimp tank - can't I just drop the eggs in the seahorse tank?" "No," she said firmly. "If a seahorse ingests part of an egg shell, it would be fatal." "What do I scoop the shrimp with," I asked. Off another shelf, she produced a mini-net. "Make sure," she added, "that you start with fresh sea water in the tank." I left the store and hustled back to the ship to tackle the brine shrimp tank problem; fortunately, my boss agreed to take that off my plate.

The following day my wife and I went to the ocean side of Coronado with buckets to collect fresh sea water. Colahan was moored in the harbor at 32nd Street, hardly a source of fresh sea water. While milling around on some rocks, in my khaki uniform, bucket in hand, trying to not slip off into the water, a Navy helicopter came buzzing by. Although he hovered overhead, wondering what I was doing, I went about my business. I really did not want to have to explain what I was doing out there to any sane person. Evelyn and I collected the water I needed as quickly as possible, loaded the full buckets into the car, and left. She said as I dropped her off, "this supply won't last long; where will you get fresh sea water next week?" I looked at her; she looked at me. Finally she said - "Oh, that's right; you'll be floating on it." Returning to the ship, I brought the water aboard, set up the tank, tested it, checked out the newly installed brine shrimp tank, and decided that I was ready to get the seahorses. I went to the store, bought the net, eggs, and the precious, little long-nosed fish. Back aboard, I very ceremoniously entered the seahorses into their new home - and dropped a few eggs into the brine shrimp tank. That evening I was like a nervous new dad, wondering if my offspring would survive the night.

When I arrived the next day, the Duty Officer informed me that the funny-looking recruits that I shanghaied were still swimming. I was relieved, and collected my receipts to get reimbursement from the Supply Officer. He reviewed them and handed them back to me, saying: "When the Squadron Supply Officer audits me, he'd just love to gig me for spending taxpayers' money frivolously just so you can get in good with the Captain." He was two grades senior to me - and didn't like me much. He added: "Go see the Welfare and Recreation Officer; see if he feels those funds can be used for crap like this." That last part especially irritated me on two counts. First, he knew Welfare and Rec funds were not to be spent for anything that didn't benefit the crew - these seahorses didn't benefit anyone. Second, he also knew that I WAS the Welfare and Recreation Officer as another collateral duty. I went to my desk, fingering the receipts that I had been stiffed for, and thought - maybe I'm not cut out to be a seagoing sailor.

Two weeks later, we arrived at Pearl Harbor and moored. We would take on fresh supplies and fix any problems that had arisen on the first leg of the trip to WestPac. Also, we knew the Squadron Commander would come aboard to speak with the Captain and see how the ship had fared the crossing. The Captain was almost giddy about having this opportunity to show off his Seahorse Squadron mascots. The officers were assembled in the wardroom when the Captain entered and proudly displayed his pets. The Commodore's reaction was classic - he just stared into the tank, no smile, just a perfectly blank look. The Captain broke the silence: "Ensign Lull has been in charge of the seahorses." The Commodore looked at me with what appeared to me to be an expression of sympathy in his eyes. He said: "Keep up the good work, Ensign." I was on deck when the Commodore left. As he reached the dry land end of the brow, his head was shaking from side to side. If I could put words to his thoughts they would be: *Seahorses? Seahorses? What idiot at the Bureau sent me this clown to command a man-of-war?* Well, those probably weren't his thoughts - but they were mine.

After a few days rest, we headed out for the next leg of our journey, during which we conducted a number of training exercises before stopping off at Midway Island to refuel. The next day we were underway again, en route to our first WestPac port of call, Yokosuka, Japan. By this time I had made friends with my charges and hadn't lost a single one. The Captain was happy about that so, let us say, life was good. We were moored alongside a Destroyer Tender to get some maintenance and repair work done while in port. Only two of the squadron ships were in Yokosuka at the time, and our next leg would be a solo voyage to Subic Bay in the Philippines. Before getting underway, we had received the information that a tropical storm was brewing around the Marshall Islands and heading slowly west. It wasn't a problem, but bore watching. When we went out, we headed dead east for a while, then began the journey south. The weather reports indicated that the storm was building and, at that time, appeared to be headed toward the Philippine Sea, perhaps to touch land at Luzon. In two days, the low had deepened, the wind strength grew, and the direction had turned northwest. It was now typhoon strength heading toward Taiwan; we should pass well east of the anticipated track. We changed our course to southwesterly toward the Philippines to pass behind this nasty storm.

The following day, we received a disturbing report; the typhoon had made a surprising turn to the northeast. Taiwan dodged a bullet; we didn't. Storm reporting in those days did not have the precision that we have today, and the computer models used for projecting tracts did not exist. It is not an exacting science even with the models - but in the 1950s, data available was significantly less than today, and data processing was rudimentary. In this case, Taiwan, mainland China, and Japan would be spared a scary experience; USS Colahan would not. We were not only in the path of a typhoon, we would be in the dangerous semicircle. In olden days, the cry onboard would be: "batten down the hatches!" All departments spent the day scouring their compartments to secure anything that could become a missile hazard in the height of the storm. A storm this size can do considerable damage even to a ship considerably longer than a football field - like a destroyer - and in World War II even capsized some.

As a midshipman on cruise, I had experienced a hurricane at sea - but that was aboard an aircraft carrier. With its rather broad, high bow, broad beam, and deep draft, it rode very differently from a sleek destroyer. It was a very bumpy ride. We rolled over 40 degrees when caught in the trough, and were pounded on the bow and superstructure when heading into the sea. In a high sea where waves and swell are 30-40 feet, its quite dangerous to run before the sea, that is, put the sea astern. At times, like slow motion, a large wave lifts the stern, holding the bow down, and rendering the rudder useless. The ship goes where the sea dictates, not where the conning officer wants it to go. To make matters worse, the wind from astern carries the stack gases forward, choking the men on the bridge who are trying to control the ship. Cooking is impossible, so cold rations are passed around occasionally. Needless to say, the heads are constantly busy - and messy. At night, all the problems of the day are magnified. When the ship began riding differently, we used spotlights to see if the sea had changed directions. Fortunately, we started from Yokosuka with a full load of fuel. Running out of fuel in a storm would be a disaster. Also, as fuel tanks were emptied, we flooded them with sea water to keep from riding too high in the water and losing stability.

On the whole we emerged from the experience relatively unscathed; lots of bumps and bruises from being tossed around, and some steel railings were twisted and would need to be replaced. However, when I went to the wardroom, I found that the two tanks had withstood the violent pounding that the ship had taken - but the inhabitants hadn't. The seahorses were on the surface, belly up. When I informed the Captain, he said - "OK, get rid of them and clean out the tanks." I did not conduct a burial at sea ceremony; in fact, I just flushed them down the toilet. I guess a typhoon experience reduces one's sensitivity.

So, that's my story, but let me add a post script. I have visited a middle school in Stuarts Draft, Virginia, just on the other side of the Blue Ridge, annually for the last three years. I'm there to talk poetry with their six graders. The teachers prepare them well. They have read my poetry and my bio; they know a lot about me before I arrive. They invariably use up more than half the time with questions. One question that always comes up is this - "Why did you go into submarines?" I am proud to report that not once did I blurt out - SEAHORSES!

The Escape Tower

It's always there -
hovering menacingly over the base.
The Tower, everyone calls it,
and each of us must go through it.
Walking from class to class, one can hardly ignore it.
I wonder if applying for submarine duty
was wise - or brave - or stupid.
Practicing an escape from a submerged submarine,
actually a sunken submarine,
how useful is that?
When they go down - they stay down.
Who needs escape training?
But, I must face the inevitable;
today's the day.

* * * * * * * * * * * * * * * * *

Ten of us crowd into the lock,
a steel compartment, cluttered with pipes and valves,
and a large door to the Tower,
fifty feet below the surface of the water.
The instructor undogs the door;
laws of physics keep it shut.
A valve is opened, and water swirls around my feet,
past my ankles, my knees, my hips, my stomach.
Visions of my panic at the Cove fifteen years before
challenge my resolve to remain calm.
Flooding stops with water nearly chin deep.
The whoosh of air and sharp pain in my ears
signal pressurizing the compartment
until the door swings open.
A nod from the instructor says my turn has come.
With three deep breaths I duck through the door,

inflate my life preserver, blow air from my lungs,
and launch myself toward the surface -
blowing all the way.
What is taking so long?
I need some air -
NOW -
and then I break the surface.
Suppressing the rush of relief,
I maintain my tranquil act.
No need to expose my fears now;
I passed the test -
I would be a submariner -
I made it!

Troubled Waters

Skipping breakfast, I left our Coronado apartment,
walked briskly to the garage, and headed out
to Orange Avenue to catch the next ferry.
Razorback was moored at the Naval Station,
and I was scheduled to get the submarine
underway for operations at eight o'clock.

As I pulled my car into the ferry line,
I turned on the radio and heard the reports
of the earthquake off Alaska and the tsunami
heading down the West Coast and toward Hawaii.
No tsunami had ever come ashore in San Diego
and done damage, but it could create weird currents.

The ferry was late and the line of cars built;
I was wedged in and could not take the longer,
alternate route down the Strand via Imperial Beach.
When the ferry arrived, it made a modified crash
landing, and the pilot stomped off, amid a marvelous
string of curse words, swearing he would not venture
out into the harbor again that day. Fortunately,
another pilot agreed to give it a try. The trip across
had interesting twists and turns, but made it.

I sped south to 32nd Street, in the Naval Station gate,
and on to the submarine pier. On board, I donned
my wash khakis, and climbed to the bridge. The exec
was anxiously awaiting me - and delivered
a few choice words for me before turning the conn
over. I took in the lines and backed away from
the pier. Without incident, we headed
into the channel, fair for leaving.

As we passed the ferry lanes, none were in sight; the one I rode was the last one that dared to cross that morning. As we were passing the sonar school, without warning, the submarine turned sharply right, ninety degrees, heading directly for shore. I backed the engines full with hard left rudder. *Razorback* shuddered to a stop, just short of going aground. We had passed through a rogue current, and I finally regained control. I backed into the channel and headed out to sea. It had been a unique experience, but a career-ending grounding had been barely averted.

Figure 2-2. Lt. Ed Lull, Officer-in-Charge, USS Roncador (and part-time motion picture consultant)

Where's My Oscar?!

Having settled my family in a new home in Westminster, California, I drove to Long Beach to report to my first shore duty assignment as Officer-in-Charge, USS Roncador (SS-301). It would be a significant change in the pace of life from my previous three seagoing ships, a destroyer and two submarines, involving four lengthy deployments to the Western Pacific. Roncador was a Balao-class submarine commissioned in March 1945, then decommissioned June 1946. After spending the 1950s in mothballs, she was towed to Long Beach and established as a Reserve Training submarine. My job as OIC was to support the training and administration of two large Naval Reserve Submarine Divisions, and to maintain the submarine in good shape for training Reserves. It was winter, 1962.

In addition to the limited work space in Roncador, I had ample office space in the adjacent Naval Reserve Training Center, San Pedro. I fell into the relative monotony of shore duty routine rather quickly. However, I soon learned that my position made me the only easily identified and accessible submariner in the entire Los Angeles/Long Beach area. This was confirmed one day when my yeoman, YN-1(SS) Peter Roskopf, turned from his desk with a curious smile on his face, and said: "Call for you, Captain, I think it's some dude from Hollywood." The caller identified himself as a representative from a television studio. He had a script that he wanted to discuss with a submariner. Deep sea divers were looking for wrecks and treasure in the Philippine Sea when they encountered a sunken submarine on the bottom with its hull intact. One of the divers approaches the sub and knocks on the hull with a wrench. As he is turning away, he is startled to hear a metallic knock, apparently from inside the submarine. The caller asked - is it feasible that, if the sub hadn't completely flooded, a person could have survived from 1945? I began mentioning the lack of air, food, etc. but interrupted myself - what show is this for, I asked. He replied: "The Twilight Zone." I said: "It's perfect." Sure enough, later that year I saw the show on TV; it was excellent Rod Serling fare.

In April the following year I had a call from a large Los Angeles radio station; I had heard earlier about a submarine on the East Coast being missing. Reports that morning had been sketchy, but the radio guy had gotten later information. He said he wanted to put me on live - did I mind? Click. "I guess you know the Navy has confirmed that the Thresher sank with all hands, were you aware ..." I can't recall any more of the interview but a neighbor later told me he had heard it and it went fine. 129 men died in that imploding metal tube. Ever since, I have felt a special empathy for those who have just witnessed or learned of a tragic incident, and had a microphone thrust in their face for their reaction. I wonder if they remember what they said.

The major event of my final year in Roncador began with a phone call from a man from Universal-Review Studio. A motion picture was being shot that included a submarine sequence; they needed to ensure there were no obvious gaffs. I reported to the studio in Universal City the following morning. Being a movie buff, this was something I was really looking forward to. I was introduced to the Director, Ralph Nelson, who had gained acclaim the preceding year for taking on the direction of a low budget movie that others had rejected - and turned it into something special. The film was ***Lilies of the Field***.

I learned a few other things about the film I was to work on. Its title was ***Father Goose*** and it was starring Cary Grant, Leslie Caron, and Trevor Howard. Now I was really excited about the opportunity to actually participate (in a small way) in the filming of a major motion picture. I was particularly happy to find that I would see Cary Grant and Trevor Howard work together in a scene. However, I was sad to learn that all scenes that included Leslie Caron were "in the can." I also learned that Ralph Nelson was not the original director; he had been hired when the picture was clearly going over budget in time and cost, and had some other serious problems. What a good move it was to bring in Ralph Nelson.

We went right to work on the set of a submarine conning tower, rigged for night vision, where the scene was going be a torpedo run on a Japanese ship. As soon as I had been introduced to the actors in their Navy uniforms (these were just bit parts in the movie) I noted that they all were wearing their dolphins on the wrong side. While they were changing, I mentioned that the night vision was retained by using red lights in the conning tower; they had blue ones. One of the old prop men grunted: "When I was in the boats in '32, we used blue." He went out to get the red light lenses; man, I was on a roll. Soon after, the actors went through a dry run of the script. To my amusement, I noticed that these actors had the relevant pages of the script open but out of sight of the camera and the director. They hadn't memorized their lines, I concluded. Hmmm ... I thought - I could do that. If one of them got sick, I could easily step in and take the part. I could picture a movie magazine headline: *Navy Guy Steals Show From Cary Grant*. Didn't happen. Oh well, I digress. On with the dry run. At the end of the torpedo run, the "Captain" yelled "Fire!" The Director looked at me, and I told him the script, as written, was not the dialogue that would be used in that type of torpedo run, and "the Captain would never yell FIRE in a submerged submarine unless he saw one." We went back to the office and met the Producer, Robert Arthur; Mr. Nelson said we need to write some script. I started to feel that perhaps I was being too picky, and suggested that the only audience that would recognize the flaws in the dialogue would be other submariners. Director looked at Producer - who said: "Let's get it right." So, we wrote some script. At this point, I was amazed at how professional and flexible these gentlemen were.

Since the locale of the picture was on islands in the western Pacific, the on-location shots were being done in Jamaica, and the daily takes were flown to the studio for review. I was invited to join the Producer and Director to examine the location shots of the previous day. I was really impressed that the Producer spotted an error: the stand-in for Cary Grant was wearing the wrong color shirt (he only had two shirts in the movie) in a scene being reviewed. Considering that the scenes were not shot in sequence, spotting that kind of error meant he really had the entire motion picture in his head. That blew my concept of producers out of the water. I thought they stayed in big offices, behind big desks, calling everyone "Baby" and giving private "screen tests" to beautiful starlets. Robert Arthur did not fit that mold at all. He was a professional.

The next day, the schedule called for shooting the external shots of the submarine surfacing. We didn't go to the waterfront; rather we walked to a building that may have been a large aircraft hangar. Near the middle of it was the superstructure of a submarine mounted on a platform with wheels. Toward one end of the building was the camera set up for shooting the scene. Behind the "submarine" was a very large translucent screen; far behind the screen was a motion picture projector. While I was looking around and getting the picture of how the shooting would be done, I glanced to the side of the building where I was standing; I'm sure my jaw dropped. I asked a prop guy nearby: "Is that the original *Phantom of the opera* set?" "Yup, that's it," he answered. Suddenly, I felt that I was in the midst of filmdom history. How many movies had I seen, I wondered, contained scenes shot right where I was standing? As they were about to start shooting, the projector was turned on, and a sea scene was projected on the see-through screen behind the "submarine" so from the camera's vantage point, the "submarine" appeared to be in the ocean. The horizon rocked with a gentle motion; I realized that when we would view the shot, the horizon would be still and the ship would appear to be rocking. In the scene, the sub had just surfaced and the Captain emerged from the conning tower hatch to the bridge. To make it more realistic, water should have been splashing around. Two prop guys were standing on the hangar floor throwing buckets of water against the sub's side. That, I thought, was really rinky-dink. Did it work? Well, you'll have to see the movie and judge for yourself.

The next day we had a scene where Cary Grant was engaged in a radio conversation with Trevor Howard and, although in the movie they were many miles from each other, their sets were adjacent so the timing was easy; they could actually hear each other speaking. It was fascinating watching two real pros like Cary Grant and Trevor Howard play off one another - but I noted the wisdom of Ralph Nelson. He knew the talent he was dealing with and he let them make the interactions work. As the scene was finishing, I heard someone holler: "TREVOR!" Trevor turned and called back: "SONNY!" There, walking onto the set was a very big, very red-faced Sonny Tufts. Apparently they were old drinking buddies and hadn't seen each other for quite a while. As I watched that scene unfold, I thought - *This is really fun!*

Later, I was talking with Ralph Nelson and a couple of others, and we were naming movies that had Cary Grant and submarines in them. They were trying to figure whether Cary Grant had more time in subs than I did. The movie that nearly all of them seemed to have enjoyed the most was **Operation Petticoat**. There were only two who had not seen the movie: I was one, Ralph Nelson was the other. In another discussion with the director, I asked him what his hopes were for the picture. He was optimistic; he explained that there were months of hard work ahead in the splicing and cutting of film to ensure a smooth flow of the plot and that the story is well-told. However, if finished in time, his hope was that it might be picked to be the Christmas show at Radio City Music Hall.

As my time on the project was winding down, Ralph Nelson made a very generous offer and I jumped on it. It was for an outing the following Saturday. Pete and Nuana Roskopf and Evelyn and I arrived at the Universal-Review Studios Saturday afternoon where Mr. Nelson had set up a tour of the lot for us. We saw many familiar sets on the tour, but the only one I specifically recall is Gilligan's Island. After the tour we went to a Chinese restaurant nearby where we met with Ralph Nelson; he treated us to dinner. Then we returned to the studio and entered the review room that I had been in days earlier. The chairs were heavily padded with an ash tray built into the arm of each. Being a smoker then, I appreciated that feature. The projectionist was ready; we sat back, relaxed, and enjoyed our private showing of **Operation Petticoat**. A delightful evening.

A month or so later, I had orders to be Navigator in USS Tench in Groton, Connecticut. We hustled across country so I could be read into the security aspects of a cruise I would be leaving on in days. It was one of those cruises where we disappear from sight, unable to communicate, then reappear somewhere in the North Atlantic months later. Returning before Christmas, I found that **Father Goose** was indeed selected to be the Christmas Show at Radio City. Evelyn and I decided to drive to New York and see it during Christmas week. We took the harrowing drive into New York City to Radio City and, upon arrival, noted that the line to get in was at least two blocks long; the wait would be hours. Reluctantly we decided to turn around and go home.

Then, Navy life got in the way, and I didn't see the movie until a few years later - aboard ship. I read the promotional pamphlet that came with the movie and learned for the first time that **Father Goose** had won one Academy Award - for screenplay. So the Academy had liked the script. Wait a minute, I wrote a part of that script. **Hey! Where's my Oscar!!!**

Christmas Party

As a member of the submarine **Tench**,
we were experiencing an early cold winter.
I was very pleased to receive
an invitation to a Christmas party.
My boss was the sub's Captain;
his boss was the Division Commander;
his boss was the Squadron Commander,
a senior Captain, aspiring to flag rank.
The Squadron Commander invited us.

It was a dress-up, catered affair,
with delightful heavy hors d'oeuvres,
and various beverages, including
a well-spiked egg nog -
a happy way to open the season.

We didn't want to overstay, so
as the party began to wind down,
we eased toward the front door,
where our hostess was stationed.
Evelyn said, "Thank you so much,
the egg log was denicious."
I followed that with, *We had
a wonderful time, Virginia.*

As we got out on the cold sidewalk,
Evelyn asked, "Did I just say that
the egg log was denicious?"
Yes, you did.
"Did you say a good-bye to Virginia?"
Certainly.
"Her name is Carolyn!"
We walked on in silence for a while.
"We probably won't be invited next year, will we?"
Probably not.

Figure 2-3. Ed and Evelyn – Party-goers

Just Getting There Was Half the Fun

It was a rather gloomy fall morning when we drove from our home in Groton, across the bridge over the Thames, to the tender in New London where USS Halfbeak was berthed. Another deployment was to begin at 8 o'clock, this one to the Mediterranean. Normally I would look forward to another adventure, but this was the fifth multi-month deployment in the two years since I drove Evelyn and our three little ones across our beautiful land from the sunny climes of Southern California. I felt a lot of guilt about leaving Evelyn once more to face a Connecticut winter with three small children. But, that's what I did for a living. LCDR Arthur Stanley Moreau, Jr. was the Commanding Officer; I was his Executive Officer.

After backing clear of the submarine tender, the Officer of the Deck eased Halfbeak into the safe channel of the Thames, heading south toward Long Island Sound, and thence through Block Island Sound, around Montauk Point to the broad Atlantic Ocean. The first day of a deployment is usually a quiet time; the crew being rather subdued as they get back to the routines of at-sea life during the boring ocean transit, wondering what adventures lie ahead for them in the ensuing months.

The third day out, we were in the Gulf Stream; the weather and the water were warm and pleasant. The Captain announced Swim Call, and we manned our stations. The OD killed the way; the Chief of the Boat, Master Chief Andy Anderson, was in charge of keeping things safe on deck. I stationed myself on the bridge as a safety observer with the ship's sharpshooter alongside, with his M-1 rifle and a full clip. After about a half hour, I announced the end of the swim. As the swimmers were climbing aboard, the Captain appeared on deck in swim trunks and goggles. He called up to me that he was going to jump in and do a visual inspection of the sonar dome. I resisted telling him what a weird idea I thought that was - and over the side he went. He swam to the bow, took a few deep breaths, and plunged. Less than five seconds later, the port lookout called, "Shark!" The OD responded, "Holy shit!" The shark was 30 yards off the port beam and not approaching; the sharpshooter raised his rifle to sight in. I directed him not to shoot unless I said to - and had the lookouts scan the waters to see if any others were around. Then we waited the nervous seconds until the Captain reappeared. As his head bobbed to the surface, the COB gestured and shouted "Shark!" The skipper fairly flew to the ladder and onto the deck. The 1MC announced, "Now secure from swim call; rig ship for dive." The incident was over; the transit continued.

Figure 2-4. LCDR Ed At Work

Two days later, we scheduled some diving officer training, spreading the word through the boat so men wouldn't be alarmed with sudden angles. It also serves as a warning to secure anything loose that might become a missile hazard. We initially went to periscope depth, 58 feet at the keel. The Captain took the conn and began running the training; he took great joy in turning this 24-year old submarine into a slow-moving roller coaster. I always position myself in the control room; it is just below the conning tower and above the pump room. That is where the Diving Officer positions himself, just behind the bow and stern plane operators. To his right is the hydraulic manifold operator; to his left is the trim manifold operator. They are on the port side. Behind the Diving Officer, on the starboard side is the air manifold operator. These are all critical stations while the submarine is submerged. In qualifying for submarines, I had learned how to operate all of these stations in routine situations and in emergencies. That is why I stationed myself there while the Captain is teasing the Diving Officers into using larger angles to change depth.

Consider a few numbers: our test depth was 412 feet; we seldom operated below 250 feet keel depth; the depth sensor was just forward of amidships; the submarine was 306 feet in length. If you pass 200 feet with a down angle of 15 degrees, what is the depth of the bow? That may seem like an innocent academic question, but on this day, on this dive, that is where we were when a loud **pop** was heard followed by the **whoosh** of flooding water, then **thwack**, like a rifle shot in the control room. "All stop - all back full" called the Captain, "Get me up!" Already the Diving Officer had ordered full rise on both planes and called, "shut the vents" to the hydraulic manifold operator. "Blow bow buoyancy" the Diving Officer called to the air manifold operator; then "blow main ballast." Quickly the angle changed to an up angle; the Captain ordered "all stop, all ahead full." As we careened upward, I told the Diving Officer, "don't use the blower." We broke the surface with a significant up angle, then the bow came slamming down as we leveled off. "All stop," the Captain ordered. The emergency was over.

Let me interrupt the story to provide a bit of explanation so the casualty and the actions will make sense. A submarine submerges by flooding its ballast tanks that are located outside the pressure hull and are open to the sea at the bottom. At the top are large lines that lead to vent valves. Water cannot enter the tanks unless the air in the tank is vacated. When the vents are opened by the hydraulic manifold operator, the air escapes, the tanks flood quickly, and the sub goes beneath the surface. To surface, the vents are shut, and 600-pound air is fed into the tanks to blow the water out the open ports at the base. However, as the sub breaks the surface the compressed air is preserved by starting the low pressure blower (located in the pump room) that delivers large volumes of air at 10 psi through the blower manifold, located in the control room. This removes the residual water from the ballast tanks. The low-pressure blower lines are six inches in diameter. The manifold (and the Submarine) are protected by flapper valves that serve as check valves, that is, they permit only one-way flow.

To continue, "What happened?" the Captain asked as I climbed to the conning tower. I responded: "I believe a low pressure blower line failed and the water rushed through the line and slammed into the blower manifold - and the check valve held. I'd like to go topside with Andy and see if we can locate the failure." The Chief and I went to the bridge, then down on deck. Opening a deck access section we lowered ourselves onto the pressure hull near where the low pressure lines accessed the hull. The first one we examined was the culprit; a pressure-induced hole was obvious. What wasn't obvious was why it failed now but not on the deep test dive after the last overhaul.

The Engineer Officer, the COB (Chief of the Boat), the Captain, and I met in the wardroom to consider our options. For the Captain, this was big. A submarine that cannot submerge, cannot complete missions and should not be at sea. If he were to be ordered to return to port, another submarine would be sent to sea on short notice to replace Halfbeak. Unfair as it may sound, the very promising career of Art Moreau would suffer a heavy hit. Never mind the cause, he would be known as the skipper whose submarine couldn't complete its mission.

"Do you have 3-M repair products on board," I asked the Engineer. "The epoxy stuff and glass wrap? Yes." I said, "Captain, I had experience using this material when I was Engineer Officer aboard Pomodon. It is incredibly strong. I'd like to try a temporary repair." "Did you use it where it is exposed to the sea under pressure?" he asked. "No sir." He was silent, staring off into space. He got up; "do it," he said and went to his stateroom.

An engineman and an electrician, both of whom had used the product (but not for this purpose), reviewed the instructions with me. We discussed the best way to adapt it to this purpose. When we reached agreement, we went topside and made the repair. Upon completion, I reported to the Captain the time needed for the material to cure and set. We continued our transit on the surface that night. In the morning I reported that the repair appeared to be complete. He went topside with me to inspect the work. It looked like an over-zealous mother's bandage of a skinned knee. He felt it, knocked on it, then smiled and said, "Let's go."

Once below, he said, "Prepare the ship to dive. I want the Engineer (who was the ship's Diving Officer) on the dive." This was vintage Art Moreau. He would not live with demons; he would fearlessly face them down, then move on to the next one. "Dive, dive" came over the 1MC, "Make your depth 5-8 feet" the Captain called to the Diving Officer. The dive was routine. After a few minutes at periscope depth, he ordered, "Make your depth 100 feet." I effected a casual calm as we descended; fortunately, no one could measure my heart rate or blood pressure. When the depth gauge read 100, and nothing untoward occurred, I began to breathe easier. "1-5-0 feet" came from the conning tower. Down we went, slowly, with a gentle angle. Eventually we arrived at that depth - and nothing happened. After a few minutes, the Captain returned to 100 feet, took a good sonar sweep, and ascended to periscope depth. After surfacing, he set the regular watch and we continued the transit. When we met in the passage way of the forward battery compartment, Captain Moreau said, "Tell all diving and conning officers that I am restricting our depth to a maximum of 150 feet for the remainder of the transit." I replied "Aye, Captain," then asked,"You didn't report this, did you?" With a sly smile, he ducked behind the curtain to his stateroom without answering.

The ocean crossing ended at Rota, Spain, where we moored alongside the submarine tender. The first one off the ship was the Captain to call on a friend who was the Repair Officer on the tender. From here on, I have nothing to report first hand, but I surmise that the Captain first was assured that the tender could affect permanent repairs to our problem before a formal report was made. Delays in reporting such a casualty would have cost many commanding officers their commands - but the aggressive (and successful) way this was handled resulted in no punitive action. In fact, I think it just enhanced his reputation. Art Moreau succeeded in all the positions he held - but not through caution - or even following all the rules. He was a throwback to the World War II submarine skippers who amazed the Navy with their exploits and their successes; he lived on the edge. Many years later, when the Iran-Contra incident broke open, it was no surprise to me to learn that the NATO Commander for Eastern Europe and Commander, Naval Forces, Mediterranean was a 4-star Admiral, Arthur Stanley Moreau, Jr. To this day, I have to believe that he was in on it; it would have been the type of secret operation he would have loved.

However, on December 8, 1986, in Naples, he suffered a heart attack and died - at age 55, leaving his wife Katie and 5 children. What a loss!

But, I digress. Repairs were completed in Rota and, once again Halfbeak put to sea. I could continue with other tales, but, well, some other time. As I mentioned at the outset, **just getting there was half the fun.**

A Special Christmas

The festive lights of Christmas
broke the wall of darkness
as we arrived at the appointed hour.
The three of us were shone in,
ushered through a long hallway,
and into the dimly-lit chapel.
In our pew, we exchanged glances,
but said nothing.

Three Naval officers, submariners,
were about to share the beauty
of the celebration of Midnight Mass
with the royal couple, in the palace
of the principality of Monaco. Our
invitations had been delivered as
our submarine moored in the harbor
days before.

Prince Ranier and Princess Grace entered,
nodded to their guests, then knelt in their pew.
I have attended Masses in many beautiful
churches and cathedrals, but this celebration
of The Feast of the Nativity in a relatively
simple chapel had the aura of welcoming,
fitting for the birth being commemorated.
While other members of our crew were
enjoying the bright lights and activities
of Monte Carlo, I was experiencing
a quiet evening to remember
for a lifetime.

Following Mass, we were led into a dining room
with a long table and a large, decorated tree
with gifts underneath. We were seated with a few
other guests, and were treated to a delightful
supper and conversation. As interested as we were
in their lives, they seemed fascinated with
the lives of their American submariner guests.

After supper, Princess Grace presented each guest
with a gift from under the tree. She gave me
a silk tie from Simpson of Piccadilly (which I wear
only on special occasions). For a Christmas
away from home, that was indeed special.

The Present

Two weeks before the event,
my wife informed me that our daughter
had told her what she wanted
for her tenth birthday.
With a crooked smile she said:
"She wants a horse;
I'll let you handle it."

For years we had drifted from place to place,
wherever the Navy said to go.
Handling any pet would by difficult -
but a horse! Our daughter was a joy,
a sweet and lovable child,
one you always want to please.
This would be a challenge.

The day came and the celebration was on.
At one point, when gift opening was underway;
I slipped out of the room.
When I returned, the birthday girl looked up
and with a huge smile she ran to me.
With her hands she gently relieved me
of the all-gray kitten and cuddled her under her chin.
"I love her, Daddy, what's her name?"
"Misty," I replied.
My wife just shook her head and murmured:
"Oh, you are devious!"

Incomplete Spring

Tiny waves, sparkling in Long Island sun,
shushed across the sand.
Tepid breezes carried scents of the new-born season.
Manly oaks ignored
the chartreuse doilies emerging
from their barren boughs. Golden-glow forsythia
along the parkway waved a welcome
as I headed toward the "home."
Everything around me proclaimed
Spring's grand awakening -

except my Dad.
Whether the alcohol or the accident carved
that gaping hole in his memory I didn't know.
Reluctantly I had acknowledged that I was in the section
that was gone forever.
Although friendly and lucid as we conversed,
he didn't know me as his son.
Our visit went well; he enjoyed my company.
On a branch beyond the open window,
an indigo bunting warbled its joyful-season song.
My Dad, a devoted lover of tree and sea, bird and flower,
didn't notice.

Figure 2-5. Richard Adelbert Lull and Son Ed

Trouble on the Trail

I pulled the station wagon into the parking area
and my two sons and I began unpacking
camping gear. Ed was a Star Scout
and Senior Patrol Leader; Jim had
recently joined the troop. This was
the favorite camporee of the year,
at the site on the Rappahannock River.

We divided the equipment so no one was
overloaded, but each pulled his own load.
It was a hike from the parking area,
across a field, through woods, then
down a hill toward the site on the river.
I selected a path and led the way.

At a point where the path took a turn
to the left, I suddenly found my face
about one foot from an extra-large pizza-sized spider web,
with an ominous, evil-looking field spider guarding its home.
One more step and I would have stumbled
into its lair. The gut-twisting terror
I had experienced thirty-five years earlier
on my cellar steps revisited me.

Summoning all the restraint I had developed
through my submarine career, I casually
pointed to my right and said:
"Let's take that path."
So we took the alternate route.
I am quite certain that my sons
never realized the trauma
that I had just experienced,
but that's what Dads are supposed to do -
isn't it?

On My Mother's Passing

We spoke in hushed and muted tones,
disjointed thoughts about the past.
Our efforts to block out the truth
through aimless conversation failed.

The moans from upstairs pierced the night
and jarred our senses into silence.
Dear Lord, her whole life has been Yours;
take her now; give her peace.

A simple, small, but sturdy woman,
unflagging and fulfilling faith defined her life.
Despite hard times, she bore and raised her five;
wealth and ease were never hers to keep.

Just months ago - it seems like years,
her cancer struck and spread like flames.
First her lungs, then her brain;
her sentence harsh with no appeal.

She accepted fate with all the grace
that made her life so blessed.
This son could not be so benign,
his faith severely tested.

The torment of the night went on;
cries of agony were knives
thrust coarsely in my chest.
Is this final penance hers or mine?

At last the drugs took full effect;
she fell into relaxed repose.
Her loving heart was also strong,
delaying this, her final voyage.

My Mother didn't die that night;
she fought for life, but won just days.
She was prepared to meet her Lord,
and died with courage as she lived.

Figure 2-6. Marybelle Brooks Lull and Son Ed

The Ballad of Deliverance
or Dropping a Daughter Off at College

"Sunny, hot, and humid" blared
The radio upstairs.
This August date I hardly cared,
So wrapped up in my prayers.

The year - a long, long time ago,
Our daughter was, at last,
Packing for the trip, you know,
The time has gone so fast.

Acceptance at her school of choice
Seemed wonderful in June;
I hardly think I shall rejoice
This summer afternoon.

A loaded car; it's time to go,
For Williamsburg we're bound.
The conversation seemed to flow,
But we were tightly wound.

The temperature was ninety-four
When we reached Barrett Hall.
"I'll carry stuff, you get the door,"
"*Be careful not to fall.*"

Unloading took an hour plus,
The sweat was flowing free.
Twas then the roommates greeted us,
I was a sight to see.

Parents talked and roommates shared;
"That one's an extrovert."
We wondered if she were prepared;
My head began to hurt.

One roommate asked, "What's your I.Q.?"
My stomach churned a bit.
The time to leave had come, I knew,
There's no avoiding it.

Goodbyes are hard and always lead
To tears and trite expression.
We cannot bring the depth we need
To offset the depression.

We drove and left our pride, our joy,
Defenseless, as it were.
*"I hope you saw that dark haired boy!
The way he looked at her!!"*

My wife was silent then for good,
A tear leaked from her eye.
We knew we'd done the best we could,
She'd earned her wings to fly.

Figure 2-7. Commander Ed Awarded a Medal

BITS AND PIECES

Part Three

The Later Years

The Hardwood Ball

My vantage point,
a second level screened-in porch,
my throne, a rocking chair.
The sky, heavy and foreboding;
the swishing sound of wind now building
into an angry growl.
So *you* are Isabel -
let's see if you can scare me inside!

The two great oaks in back
threaten me,
but they have sneered at storms before.
The nearest one, like a telephone pole
with fringe on top.
Its partner shows much more life up high.
These two sentinels dwarf
pines, beeches, and hollies in their flock.

Wind has now matured,
roaring like full-throttle raceway cars.
The steady force now punctuated
by blasting gusts.
My oaks have begun their eerie dance:
the pole an uneven sway, a line dance
back and forth with jerky bows;
the other with heavy growth up high
adds twists and turns, and sudden dips -
a tango tree.

As winds reach their height, I sense
my monster dancers will see the prom
to its end.
Suddenly, an interloper from a neighbor's yard,
a beech, makes its attack.
It heads directly at me, but

        crashes just short of my perch.
              As time passes
   the roar becomes somewhat less intense.
         My yard - a disaster,
   my tall friends dance a little slower;
        the worst has passed.
              I rock on.

The Love-Hate Game

My love for the golf course I don't understand.
I spend so much time in the woods and in sand.
I see great improvement each time on the range,
but then when I play my score just doesn't change.

No matter what part of my game that goes well,
a leveling force casts its score-killing spell.
When hitting my driver with all sorts of power,
my chipping goes nowhere - my putting goes sour.

I think that my partners just take me along
to be an example of what can go wrong.
My handicap should let me win on occasion,
but I've yet to locate that winning equation.

*   *   *   *   *   *   *

Wow! Look at that drive, it's so long and so straight;
my love for this game I cannot overstate.

A Dizzy Day

Walking out to get my morning paper,
suddenly I turned right onto the grass.
Don't know why I turned -
I tried to turn back -
my balance was askew -
the world swirled around me -
reached for the paper -
it almost got away from me -
tried to reach the front door erect -
took baby steps with feet wide apart -
must have looked like pathetic drunk -
finally I made it.

Later, at the hospital,
they took those very noisy pictures
of my brain.
By that time, I was able to walk
a straight line.

Later, I asked:
"What did the MRI show of my brain?"
"It was normal," he responded.
I ignored the unintended put-down:
"No stroke?" "No stroke."
"So, what's next?"
"If it happens again, come directly to the ER."

I left the hospital harboring an unsolved mystery
with the ominous feeling that if this poem
merits another, follow-on verse,
someone else will have to write it.

Joyless Journey

The compact Ford hummed along at 70
en route Orlando to Vero Beach.
Conversation aimed at keeping upbeat
failed to mask the somber purpose of the journey.
Our previous visit was a happy occasion,
but not this time.
Moods have changed, as has the landscape.

My brother and his valiant wife faced first
the strife of one great tempest
that drove them from their darkened home.
The gaping hole in the roof could not be covered
before the second vicious blow brought nature's wrath inside.
Coping with disaster was too much for his damaged heart.
As quiet Christmas passed, he did as well.

The further south we went, the sadder the scene.
Once stately, supple palms now snapped
or nearly free of fronds.
Telephone poles lying in ditches, wires limp;
neighborhoods dotted with blue tarps
covering unrepaired roofs;
damaged buildings sitting dark and vacant.

Entering my brother's neighborhood
the weight of tragic loss surrounded us.
The once perky and vibrant environment
with its well-kept homes and tailored lawns
was now silent, perhaps mourning its losses.

My brother's home, and others, are unlivable;
filled with slime and mold.

When war and politics and other events
replace natural disasters as news,
we forget what has been left behind.
Years from now the scars will still remain;
many saw their dreams and fortunes blown away.
Some damaged items - like my brother's heart -
could never be repaired.

The Leader

An elegy honoring Richard Gilbert Lull

He blazed life's trails as leaders often do,
appearing to have guidance from above,
defining family in moral terms
of loyalty, commitment, faith and love.

This first-born son emerged in troubled times
where life's most precious lessons were begun.
He served his country selflessly in war
and then came home to his young wife and son.

They built a life admired by those they knew;
their home with five young boys, was truly blessed.
This simple rule brought joy and happiness:
that family comes first - then all the rest.

And now he leads again with quiet grace
to walk the road we all must take one day.
His confidence and courage make us strong;
when our time comes, he will have shown the way.

My Oval Landscape

The stands are board-hard, unforgiving seats
where anxious parents, friends, and fans collect
to watch and cheer for track athletes who know
that head and legs and heart must now connect.

Like most, I have my stopwatch in my hands;
my eyes are focused on the starter's gun.
As runners toe the line, a nervous hush;
my thumb awaits the flash to start the run.

* *

Her blonde hair, pony-tailed, flew arrow-straight
then bobbed in sync with obstacles below.
With picture form, she soared with grace and ease;
no hurdles in her lane received a blow.
This little girl knew her success required
agility and speed, not strength and size.
At race's end, she wore the winning tape,
then on the platform, claimed her golden prize.

No natural athlete was this fair-skinned boy
who trained as hard as any I had seen.
Exhausting workouts soon produced results
as PRs came to be almost routine.
At six feet, lean, he had an upright style
and loved to run in front and lead the pack.
He left his school the middle distance king;
the one who looked ahead and never back.

A skilled performer in 'most any sport,
he tried the track to see if he would fit.
No burning speed, he chose the distance runs:
success defined by stamina and grit.
Cross country soon became his running forte;
he trained on hills in weather cold and damp,
but he was well-prepared for his big race.
This harrier became the county champ.

* *

That generation all became adults
so many years ago - but in my mind
the scenes are just as clear as if they were
the movies of my dreams I could rewind.

The thrill of competition is renewed,
with nervousness I hardly can ignore.
As children of my children toe the line,
my oval landscape comes alive once more.

Figure 3-1. Grandchildren and Others Await the Gun

Echo(of a)cardiogram

I saw my heart today,
and my mind gamboled in a dozen different directions.
It wasn't a brilliant red valentine,
with symmetrical shape and smooth curves.
Actually, it seemed rather amorphous.
It doesn't look like a container
that holds a lifetime of love.

When I offer someone 'heartfelt thanks'
I don't think it relates to that critter on the screen.
When I am speaking 'from the heart'
I am certain it is not from that relentless pump.
Ever notice how often 'heart' and 'soul'
appear in the same sentence or song verse?
I saw my heart today; didn't see my soul.

That blob on the screen was working -
I mean REALLY working hard.
Every second or so - lub dub - lub dub - lub dub.
It's been beating that incessant rhythm
for every minute of every hour of every day
of every month for nearly eighty years.
At night I rest; it never rests.

I saw my heart today:
lub dub - lub dub - lub dub.
It was awesome; it was eerie.
My very life depends
on that tireless engine of repetitive action.
I wanted to stand up and cheer for it;
perhaps a prayer would be more appropriate.

Fairway Folly

My game wasn't going badly
for a cold February morning
as I approached hole number 13,
my nemesis, on the Black Heath course.
You won't defeat me this time, I thought.
After a fair drive and an OK 6-iron lay-up shot,
I found myself just wedge distance from the green.
I was going around the water, not over it.
However, my lob-wedge failed to lob;
swinging with needless haste, I miss-hit,
sending my white ball skittering
across the dormant Bermuda grass,
quickly out of my short-sighted vision.

Approaching the green, pulling my push-cart
between bunker and pond bank,
I did not spot my ball where I expected
to encounter it. *Could it have kicked left
into the sand*? Releasing my cart, I took
one step left to peek into the bunker.
The sound of club-heads clinking together
caused me to spin around to see
my cart, bag, and clubs careening
down the bank toward the pond.
I stood motionless, mouth agape,
like a helpless doofus, and watched
as my golfing essentials took one final bounce,
and belly-flopped into the pond.
As the cart slid beneath the surface,
only part of one wheel remained
above the surface - gasping for air.

Following an extended moment
of embarrassing silence, a golfing partner -
I shall call him hero-man - said, "I can get it."
After removing his shoes and socks,
he stepped gingerly into the frigid water
that had a layer of ice five days earlier.
He began retrieval operations
that took ten foot-numbing minutes.
"Is everything there," he asked?
"All but my 7-iron," I responded, hesitatingly.
Back in he went, and fished out the prodigal club.
The only casualty of the incident
was a water-logged antiquated cell phone.

After dumping water from golf bag pockets,
I opted to do what every avid golfer would do:
continue the round.
I announced that I would drop on the bank
where my ball had apparently gone
into the water (with my cart and bag in cold pursuit).
"Why," hero-man called? "You're up here."
He pointed to a prim white spheroid,
the only dry piece of golf equipment I owned,
sitting twenty feet from the pin.
At my creative best, I replied:
"Well I'll be damned."
And yes, I missed the putt.

On My 50th High School Reunion

The music was too loud!
We were there to talk, not shout.
DJs thought they nailed the tunes
from 50 years ago.
They missed!
Flapper stuff on one side;
rock and roll on the other.
Where were Perry, Doris, Bing, Jo?

My first return in all those years,
but I'd been warned.
I knew the names - but not the faces.
Surely they'd recognize me!
But when these closest friends of yore
squinted to read my label, I knew
I had not escaped the calendar's curse;
my looking glass had lied.

One hundred fourteen stories to be told,
but we waited too long for thirty.
Ron and Nick, Colleen and Sandy,
Zane and George, the Wittmann twins,
Janet, Fred - all called too soon.
Although we celebrated the wonders
of our diverse lives,
we also faced the dark.

Were old friendships rejuvenated
or just revisited?
One evening in fifty years
is not enough.
Many promises and good intentions
of graduation day had faltered years ago.
This time we relished the joy of being together;
no commitments - no regrets.

Figure 3-2. Ed and Evelyn - June 4, 1955

Figure 3-3. Ed and Evelyn - June 4, 2005

A Golden Journey

A windy, wintry day in '53
we walked above the rocks on Severn's shore.
I knew commitment time was here - and we
agreed to share our lives forevermore.

On June the fourth of 1955
we said our solemn vows and thus began
a golden journey on that joyful road
of love between a woman and a man.

The Navy kept us moving place-to-place,
and sometimes caused us lengthy times apart.
We learned the hurt of separation was
a test to the devotion of the heart.

Despite the painful loss of our first son,
our children came and claimed their share of love.
They soon became the focus of our lives;
they were most welcome gifts from God above.

In just one blink they all grew up and left
and each pursued the challenge of career.
But then in just two blinks the grandkids came;
a whole new outlet for our love was here.

And now, three blinks, and fifty years have passed -
a blur - but filled with mem'ries to recall.
Some wins, some losses, highs and lows, were ours -
but love - and only love - outlasts them all.

Happy Golden Anniversary, Evelyn,
With all my love, Ed

Mid-Winter Encounter

Loose driveway stones crackled under tires
as I approached my garage,
biting cold and dark as tar.
High beams illuminated the garage door
and newly-trimmed vitex bush.
My vision fastened
on the bulky object on branch stubs,
at eye level and motionless.
It was an owl, wings folded,
unruffled by my presence
or by being on stage, in the spotlight,
surrounded by blackness.

Emerging from the car, I stood still,
exchanging stares with this regal creature.
A large head, flat face with glistening eyes
and short, hooked beak,
sat atop a hawk-sized body
with speckled brown feathers.
Although I have heard owls at night,
I had never seen one up close.
I stood a dozen feet away, like a statue,
my sense of awe growing.
Suddenly his head swivelled,
as if on a well-oiled bearing.
Nothing seen, he resumed his curious gaze.
What thoughts danced behind those blazing eyes?
What instincts assured him I was no threat?

This marvelous bird remained placid,
until garage door creaking broke the spell,
disturbing the equilibrium of the encounter.
I experienced a strange sadness
when, with the whirr of waving wings,
he vanished into the night.

On Visiting Stuarts Draft Middle School

Ninety six beaming faces,
as only six-graders can beam,
eagerly anticipated
what I would bring to them.
They had been briefed;
they knew who I was
and why I was there.

I read a patriotic poem,
then a couple of light verses
with surprise endings.
They delighted in these poems.

Just a few minutes into the program
I asked if any one had a question.
About fifty hands flashed into the air;
they were really prepared.

The energy level in the room
pumped me up.
The quality of the questions
and the way they were asked
belied their age.
Their interest and enthusiasm
with poetry made my day.

However, nearly a third of the questions
were on the subject of submarines
and life in the undersea Navy.
Clearly, they knew more about me
than I knew about them.
When lunch period ended our hour together,
a dozen hands still waved.
I pray I filled their lives that day
the way they filled mine.

Witness to the Crime

The brilliant sun at summer's peak
warmed my shoulders as I walked
through field and forest.
Nature was at peace,
my imagination at rest.
Approaching home, I stepped
onto the road, mind wandering.

Suddenly I spotted a silent,
motionless bird, on the road,
twenty feet directly in front of me,
wings spread, seemingly dead
or injured. I froze on the spot;
by coloring and size, I recognized
the marsh hawk. This creature
is seldom a victim.

After staring briefly, I ventured
a step or two toward this bird of prey.
With one motion, he rose to full height,
sprang upward with a powerful leap,
flapped strong, broad wings,
and became airborne. Then I saw,
dangling from his talons,
a lifeless adult squirrel.

Reconstructing the scene in my mind,
I pictured the rodent crossing the road,
unaware of imminent danger,
and the silent predator swooping down,
grasping his prey, and spreading his wings
to achieve privacy. His lethal talons
swiftly finished nature's work.
I was just an accidental
witness to the crime.

The "I"s Have It

I'm not much of a poet, you see
I am a rather happy individual.
I enjoy good food and eat well;
I can afford my favorite Scotch.
I have a wonderful wife and family,
and live in a nice house and neighborhood.

I still walk the golf course and
don't sweat my score.
I have no trouble filling my time
doing things I enjoy. I have no one
saying "do this" or "do that" or
"go here" or "go there" or
"jump through a hoop."

I have loads of good, stimulating
friends who share poetry and essays.
I believe I need some good, solid
misery to spice up my writing.

Reviewing what I've written so far,
I have used the pronoun "I" twelve times.
Like I said, I'm not much of a poet,
but being that egocentric, perhaps
I should run for Congress.

I Am in Love - Again

(On meeting my first Great Granddaughter)

I held her in my arms and our eyes met.
Her calm made my heart race; no one foretold
that at this age I'd fall in love again.
Just think - my love is only six hours old!

Figure 3-4. A Fourth Generation of Love

Figure 3-5. The Children With Spouses

Figure 3-6. The Grandchildren

About the Author

Edward W. Lull was born September 2, 1932 in North Wales, Pennsylvania, where he lived until 1942, when the family moved to Greenwich, New York. In 1946 the Lull family relocated to Troy, New York; Ed graduated from Lansingburgh High School in 1950. He completed one semester at New York State College for Teachers before enlisting in the U.S. Navy in February 1951. Having received an appointment to the U.S. Naval Academy, he graduated with the Class of 1955. On June 4, 1955, he married the former Evelyn Elizabeth Palmer of Glen Burnie Maryland.

Lull's twenty years of commissioned service included sea duty aboard one destroyer and two submarines out of San Diego, two submarines out of New London, and a personnel transport in San Diego. Shore duty tours included a reserve training submarine, the Office of Naval Research, and Bureau of Naval Personnel. He earned a masters degree from The George Washington University in 1969. Lull retired from the Navy in 1975.

In his second career, Lull held management and executive positions in several small hi-tech firms in the Washington, D.C. area until 1994. He served as president and chairman of The Professional Group of Fairfax until retiring to Williamsburg in 1997.

Lull began writing poetry in retirement and he edited a book of poetry, *Vintage Wine and Good Spirits* for the Williamsburg Poetry Guild in 2000. Subsequently he published three books of his poetry: *Cabin Boy to Captain: a Sea Story* in 2003; *Where Giants Walked* in 2005; and *The Sailors: Birth of a Navy* in 2007. His activity in the Poetry Society of Virginia includes four terms as its president. He planned and hosted annual three-day poetry festivals in Williamsburg for ten years. Ed and Evelyn have three children, eight grandchildren, and one great granddaughter.

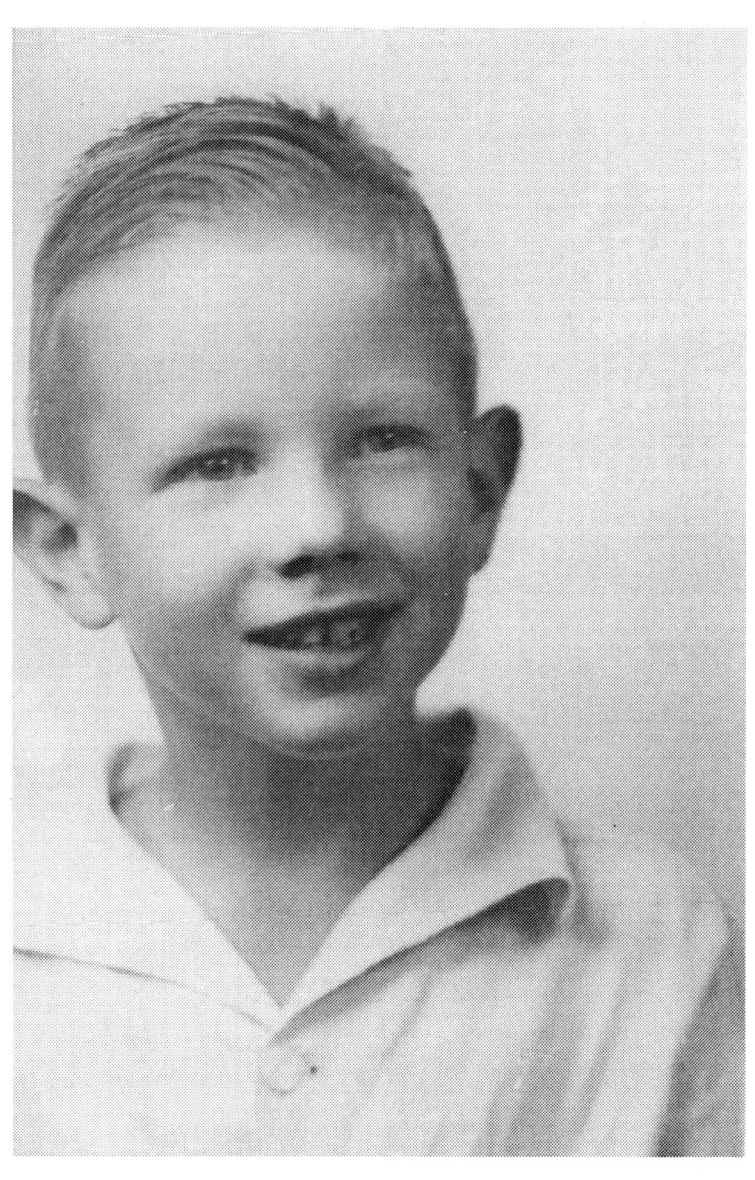

Figure 3-7. Edward Warren Lull, Circa 1937